ORT WALKS
DE EASY

OWE
SWANS BAY

Ordnance Survey

Contents

Walk 1

CWM IVY & HILLS TOR

Distance
2.2 miles / 3.5 km

Time
1½ hours

Start/Finish
Llanmadoc

Parking SA3 1DE
Whiteford Beach car
park

Cafés/pubs
Cwm Ivy Café; Britannia
Inn, Llanmadoc

**Superb coast
views to
lighthouse on a
quiet corner of
Gower**

Page 14

Walk 2	Walk 3	Walk 4
RHOSSILI & WORMS HEAD	**CEFN BRYN & ARTHUR'S STONE**	**PENNARD CLIFFS & PWLLDU HEAD**

Distance 2.7 miles/4.3km	**Distance** 5 miles/8 km	**Distance** 4.5 miles/7.2km
Time 1½ hours CATCH A BUS	**Time** 3 hours	**Time** 2½ hours CATCH A BUS
Start/Finish Rhossili	**Start/Finish** Above Reynoldston	**Start/Finish** Southgate
Parking SA3 1PR National Trust car park	**Parking** SA3 1AG Roadside car park, ½ mile east of Reynoldston	**Parking** SA3 2DH National Trust Southgate car park, East Cliff Lane
Cafés/pubs Rhossili	**Cafés/pubs** King Arthur Hotel, Reynoldston	**Cafés/pubs** Three Cliffs Coffee Shop; The Lookout

Magnificent golden sands and seal watching at Gower's tip	**One of the best ridge walks in Britain along ancient trackway**	**Gower's most rugged cliffs; delicious ice cream; lots of seabirds**

Contents **3**

Walk 5	Walk 6	Walk 7
LANGLAND TO OYSTERMOUTH CASTLE	**SWANSEA HERITAGE WALK**	**AFAN FOREST PARK**

Distance 3.5 miles/5.6km	**Distance** 2.9 miles/4.6km	**Distance** 3.6 miles/5.8km
Time 2 hours	**Time** 1½ hours	**Time** 2 hours
CATCH A BUS	GO BY TRAIN · CATCH A BUS	CATCH A BUS
Start Langland Bay **Finish** Oystermouth	**Start/Finish** Paxton Street car park	**Start/Finish** Afan Forest Park
Parking SA3 4SQ Langland Bay car park	**Parking** SA1 3SA Paxton Street car park, Swansea	**Parking** SA12 9SG Rhyslyn car park, Afan Forest, Pontrhydyfen
Cafés/pubs Langland Bay; Mumbles; Oystermouth	**Cafés/pubs** Swansea	**Cafés/pubs** Visitor centre café; Miners Arms, Pontrhydyfen

Rock pooling; lifeboat and castle heritage; seafront fish and chips	**Vibrant waterfront, eye-catching architecture and great museums**	**Attractively forested valley walk to excellent Miners' Museum**

Page 42	**Page 48**	**Page 54**

Walk 8

MARGAM COUNTRY PARK

Distance
2.6 miles/4.2km

Time
1½ hours CATCH A BUS

Start/Finish
Margam Country Park

Parking SA13 2TJ
Margam Country Park
car park

Cafés/pubs
Café at Margam Castle

Fairytale castle, abbey, gardens, deer park, lakes and farm trail

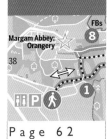

Walk 9

PARC SLIP

Distance
1.9 miles/3.1km

Time
1 hour CATCH A BUS

Start/Finish
Parc Slip Nature Reserve

Parking CF32 0EH
Parc Slip Visitor Centre
car park

Cafés/pubs
At visitor centre; The
Fountain pub

Nature walk; woods and birdsong around revitalised mining area

Walk 10

OGMORE: COAST & DOWNS

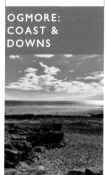

Distance
4.6 miles/7.4km

Time
2½ hours CATCH A BUS

Start/Finish
Ogmore-by-Sea

Parking CF32 0QA
Ogmore Beach car
park

Cafés/pubs
Café at West Farm;
pub at Southerndown

Fine beach, shipwreck coast, Ogmore River and Wales Coast Path

GETTING OUTSIDE
IN GOWER AND SWANSEA BAY

" spectacular cliffs and coves, once the haunt of smugglers and now prime habitat for peregrine falcons

OS Champion
Chris Knight

Southgate

A very warm welcome to the new Short Walks Made Easy guide to Gower and Swansea Bay – what a fantastic selection of leisurely walks we have for you!

Gower – Gŵyr in Welsh – was Britain's first Area of Outstanding Natural Beauty, designated in 1956. Measuring roughly 18 miles long by 5 miles wide, the rectangular-shaped Gower Peninsula juts out from the South Wales coastline between Llanelli and Swansea. Renowned for its magnificent and varied coastal scenery, the walks encompass: wide-sweeping views over the dunes of Whiteford Burrows on the quieter side of the peninsula; the rugged sea serpent-like rock formation of Worms Head from the coast path near Rhossili; and the spectacular cliffs and coves, once the haunt of smugglers and now prime habitat for peregrine falcons, from Three Cliffs Bay to Pwlldu Head.

The walks touch upon Gower's long history: Neolithic Arthur's Stone on the ancient ridge walk along Cefn Bryn, the peninsula's old red sandstone 'backbone'; the castles at Pennard and Oystermouth; and the maritime heritage of Swansea on the rejuvenated waterfront of Wales' second city.

Strolls around Mumbles and Margam Country Park, on opposite sides of the water, reveal fantastic views over Swansea Bay. High above Port Talbot and Bridgend, birdlife and wildflowers abound at Afan Forest Park and Parc Slip, where re-foresting and re-wilding make these wildlife havens unrecognizable from their industrial past.

Chris Knight, OS Champion

WE SMILE MORE WHEN WE'RE OUTSIDE

The Conygaer

Whether it's a short walk during our lunch break or a full day's outdoor adventure, we know that a good dose of fresh air is just the tonic we all need.

At Ordnance Survey (OS), we're passionate about helping more people to get outside more often. It sits at the heart of everything we do, and through our products and services, we aim to help you lead an active outdoor lifestyle, so that you can live longer, stay younger and enjoy life more.

We firmly believe the outdoors is for everyone, and we want to help you find the very best Great Britain has to offer. We are blessed with an island that is beautiful and unique, with a rich and varied landscape. There are coastal paths to meander along, woodlands to explore, countryside to roam, and cities to uncover. Our trusted source of inspirational content is bursting with ideas for places to go, things to do and easy beginner's guides on how to get started.

It can be daunting when you're new to something, so we want to bring you the know-how from the people who live and breathe the outdoors. To help guide us, our team of awe-inspiring OS Champions share their favourite places to visit, hints and tips for outdoor adventures, as well as tried and tested accessible, family- and wheelchair-friendly routes. We hope that you will feel inspired to spend more time outside and reap the physical and mental health benefits that the outdoors has to offer. With our handy guides, paper and digital mapping, and exciting new apps, we can be with you every step of the way.

To find out more visit os.uk/getoutside

THE GOWER WAY

INAUGURATED BY
HRH THE PRINCE OF WALES KG
26 JULY 1998
A GOWER SOCIETY MILLENNIUM PROJECT
AGORWYD YN SWYDDOGOL GAN
EUB TYWYSOG CYMRU KG
26 GORFFENNAF 1998
CYNLLUN MILENIWM
CYFEILLION GŴYR

LLWYBR GŴYR

RESPECTING
THE COUNTRYSIDE

You can't beat getting outside in the British countryside, but it's vital that we leave no trace when we're enjoying the great outdoors.

Let's make sure that generations to come can enjoy the countryside just as we do.

 Leave no trace

 Keep dogs under control; bin and bag waste

 Do not light fires; only BBQ at official sites

 Leave gates as you find them

 Keep to footpaths and open access land

 Plan ahead for your trip

For more details please visit
www.gov.uk/countryside-code

USING THIS GUIDE

Easy-to-follow Gower and Swansea Bay walks for all

Before setting off

Check the walk information panel to plan your outing

- Consider using **Public transport** where flagged. If driving, note the satnav postcode for the car park under **Parking**
- The suggested **Time** is based on a gentle pace
- Note the availability of **Cafés**, tearooms and pubs, and **Toilets**

Terrain and hilliness

- **Terrain** indicates the nature of the route surface
- Any rises and falls are noted under **Hilliness**

Walking with your dog?

- This panel states where **Dogs** must be on a lead and how many stiles there are – in case you need to lift your dog
- Keep dogs on leads where there are livestock and between April and August in forest and on grassland where there are ground-nesting birds

A perfectly pocket-sized walking guide

- Handily sized for ease of use on each walk
- When not being read, it fits nicely into a pocket...
- ...so between points, put this book in the pocket of your coat, trousers or day sack and enjoy your stroll in glorious national park countryside – we've made it pocket-sized for a reason!

Flexibility of route presentation to suit all readers

- **Not comfortable map reading?** Then use the simple-to-follow route profile and accompanying route description and pictures
- **Happy to map read?** New-look walk mapping makes it easier for you to focus on the route and the points of interest along the way
- Read the insightful **Did you know?**, **Local legend**, **Stories behind the walk** and **Nature notes** to help you make the most of your day out and to enjoy all that each walk has to offer

OS information about the walk

• Many of the features and symbols shown are taken from Ordnance Survey's celebrated **Explorer** mapping, designed to help people across Great Britain enjoy leisure time spent outside

OS information

🚶 SS 439935
Explorer 164

• National Grid reference for the start point
• Explorer sheet map covering the route

The easy-to-use walk map

• **Large-scale** mapping for ultra-clear route finding

• **Numbered points** at key turns along the route that tie in with the route instructions and respective points marked on the profile

• **Pictorial symbols** for intuitive map reading, see Map Symbols on the front cover flap

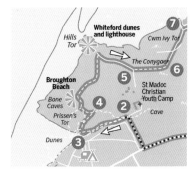

The simple-to-follow walk profile

• Progress easily along the route using the illustrative profile, it has **numbered points** for key turning points and **graduated distance** markers

• Easy-read **route directions** with turn-by-turn detail

• Reassuring **route photographs** for each numbered point

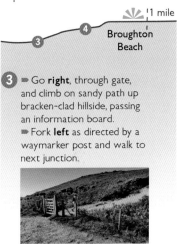

3 ➧ Go **right**, through gate, and climb on sandy path up bracken-clad hillside, passing an information board.
➧ Fork **left** as directed by a waymarker post and walk to next junction.

CWM IVY AND HILLS TOR

Set on the quieter north-west corner of Gower, nestling between the slopes of Llanmadoc Hill and the pines and dunes of Whiteford Sands, Llanmadoc offers a picturesque start to a very pretty walk. A mainly gentle climb to the headland reveals views over the sands of Broughton Beach to the distant outlines of Worms Head and, in the other direction, past Cwm Ivy Tor to an old lighthouse in the estuary just beyond the dunes of Whiteford Sands, with the hills of Carmarthenshire beyond.

OS information

🔾 SS 439935
Explorer 164

Distance
2.2 miles/3.5km

Time
1½ hours

Start/Finish
Llanmadoc

Parking SA3 1DE
Whiteford Beach car park (donation)

Public toilets
None

Cafés/pubs
Cwm Ivy Café and Crafts; Britannia Inn, Llanmadoc

Terrain
Country lanes, sandy paths, stony track

Hilliness
Gradual ascent from 🔾 to Hills Tor; moderately steep descent on sandy path beneath Cwm Ivy Tor

Did you know? The Burry Estuary was used during World War II as a shelling and mining range. After the war any unexploded bombs were cleared by the army.

Local legend It is said that the young St Cennydd was abandoned by his parents and left in a basket on the waters of the Loughor (Llwchwr) Estuary. He was rescued by gulls, which carried him to the safety of the sand dunes and fed him with their beaks as if he were one of their own. Angels came down and put a bell, known as a titty bell, in his mouth. This gave him nourishment and he grew strong. At age 18, Cennydd took himself to Llangennith, the next village to Llanmadoc, and performed many miracles.

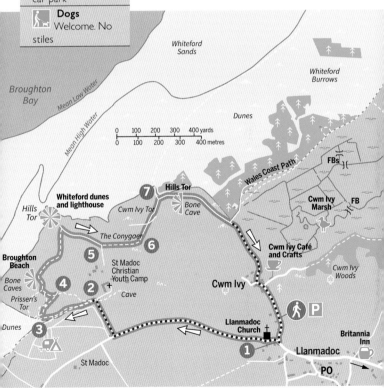

STORIES BEHIND THE WALK

✝ ■ Llanmadoc Church

The church at Llanmadoc was founded in the 6th century by St Madoc, a pupil of St David and, later, St Cennydd. It was rebuilt in the 13th century and heavily restored in the 1800s. Inside are two large stones, one a 7th-century village boundary stone and the second, the remains of an old cross. The church's font is Norman.

🐦 Cwm Ivy Marsh

Until the 17th century, Cwm Ivy Marsh was part of the extensive salt marshes of North Gower. A sea wall was then built and the reclaimed land was used to graze sheep. The new pastureland, dotted with Corsican pines and willows, held out against the tide until the winter storms of 2014, when the wall was breached. Salt water spread inland, gradually creating a salt water marsh again. While the pines and willows died, the National Trust decided to let nature take its course and today there's a flourishing wetland habitat.

✝ ■ Llanmadoc Church

🚶 ①

🅿 Whiteford Beach car park

½ mile

🔴 Leave the car park by the lane entrance and turn **left** to climb the lane to a junction.

①
🔴 Turn **right** along road, passing the church (right).
🔴 On reaching the caravan park in ½ mile, turn **right** along the lane to a right-hand bend.

⚜ Whiteford Lighthouse

Now decommissioned, the Grade II-listed Whiteford Lighthouse was designed by John Bowen and built in 1865, to mark the south side of the Loughor (Llwchwr) Estuary. Unusually, it is constructed from cast iron, the only one of its type to be built offshore. The tower is 43 feet high and can be seen clearly from Hills Tor, the high point of the route. It can also be reached on foot at low tide.

☆ The Knights Templar

Margaret, Countess of Warwick, granted the parish of Llanmadoc to the Knights Templar around 1156. This was a powerful Catholic military order whose headquarters were on Temple Mount, Jerusalem. The Templars were closely linked to the Crusades – they helped Christian pilgrims travel freely through the Holy Land. When the Holy Land was lost, support for them waned and they suffered much persecution throughout Europe. Pope Clement disbanded the order in 1312. Llanmadoc and its church passed to the Knights Hospitallers, who later became the St John's Ambulance.

2 ➡ On lane bend at the back of caravan park, fork **left** and follow a sandy path rising gently away from caravans to reach path junction with gate on right.

3 ➡ Go **right**, through gate, and climb on sandy path up bracken-clad hillside, passing an information board.
➡ Fork **left** as directed by a waymarker post and walk to next junction.

Broughton Beach

1 mile

NATURE NOTES

The dunes bordering the sandy beaches of Broughton and Whiteford are a special feature of the area, part of a national nature reserve. Here you'll find creeping willow, a squat shrub that survives well in the ever-shifting sands. It does this by sending out low shoots that creep along the surface of the sand. Miner bees (there are over 20 species here) can be seen feeding on the willow's pale yellow flowers. Any bracken on the dunes is cut back regularly to stop it taking hold. The common lizard, slow worm, grass snake and adder thrive here. The vivid pinks of bloody cranesbill and pyramidal orchids add colour to the scene. They love the calcium-rich, sandy soils. Looking to the skies, you may well see hovering kestrels.

Pyramidal orchids

Hills Tor
(Whiteford dunes and lighthouse, north)

⑤

⑥

1½ miles

⑦

④ ➡ Take the **left** fork through a gate indicated by another waymarker post and climb to Hills Tor.
➡ Continue on path round the headland to a bench and information board.

⑤ ➡ Just beyond bench, take the **leftmost** of two gates and follow path through trees.
➡ Path soon descends quite steeply but only for a short way, becoming sandy again and gradually less steep to reach marker post at a fork.

Creeping willow

Slow worm

Bloody cranesbill

Common lizard

Cwm Ivy Café
and Crafts

Cwm Ivy
Tor

Cwm Ivy Marsh (left)

2 miles

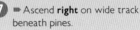

Whiteford Beach car park 🅿

6 ➡ Fork **left** (waymarked) as path descends towards a firing range.
➡ Keep **right** of the range. Go through the gate at the bottom.

7 ➡ Ascend **right** on wide track beneath pines.
➡ Stay with it, rising to Cwm Ivy, past the café, then through a gate out onto the lane.
➡ Follow the lane uphill before turning **left** into car park.

CATCH A BUS

OS information

⬤ SS 414880
Explorer 164

Distance	2.7 miles/4.3km
Time	1½ hours
Start/Finish	Rhossili
Parking SA3 1PR	National Trust car park
Public toilets	By National Trust information centre at far end of car park
Cafés/pubs	Rhossili
Terrain	Firm paths, tracks and lanes

RHOSSILI AND WORMS HEAD

Rhossili Down plunges to the 3-mile sandy beach at the end of the Gower Peninsula. This creates a spectacular sight, especially when the sea breeze is making white horses on the waves. Worms Head, a rugged 'serpent' of sharp rocks jutting into the sea, is an island at high tide. This route rounds the clifftops to pass 'the Worm' then peers into Fall Bay before a cross-pasture return to Rhossili. If the tide's out, take a stroll along Rhossili sands to see the skeletal wreck of the ship, *Helvetia*.

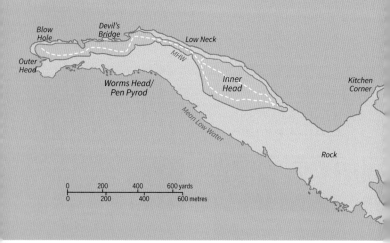

Hilliness
Gently undulating

Footwear
Year round 👢

Public transport
Bus service 118 from Swansea: traveline.cymru

Accessibility
All-terrain wheelchairs and pushchairs to the Lookout Station, **2**

Dogs
Welcome but keep on leads due to livestock. No stiles

Local legend The ghost of Reverend John Ponsonby Lucas has been seen descending the stairs of the old Rhossili Rectory, the white house at the foot of Rhossili Down. He has also appeared immaculately dressed in his Edwardian clothes riding his galloping black stallion across the sands. On stormy nights the sands are also said to be haunted by Squire Mansell, who rides in a fine black coach pulled by four grey horses. The squire is said to be searching for gold buried in the sands.

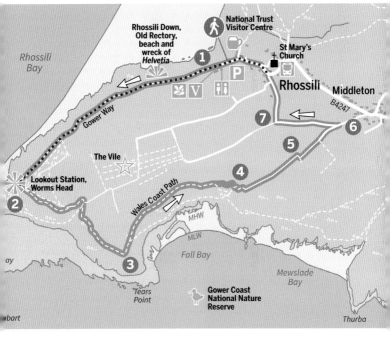

STORIES BEHIND THE WALK

☆ *Helvetia* At low tide you'll see the oak skeleton of the Norwegian barque, *Helvetia*, which got into trouble around Mumbles and was stranded here in 1887. All the crew survived, as did the cargo, but five men from the salvage crew were drowned when their boat capsized.

⚑ St Mary's Church

In the 6th century a church was built beneath Rhossili Down near the sands, but is believed to have been ravaged by storms sometime in the 13th century. St Mary's Church, built to replace it, lies at the top of the village. The church has a fine ornately carved Norman archway. Historians believe it comes from the original church. There's also a memorial to local man, Petty Officer Edgar Evans, who died on Captain Scott's ill-fated mission to Antarctica in 1912.

National Trust car park

Rhossili Down, Old Rectory, beach and wreck of *Helvetia*

½ mile

➤ Go through one of the car park gateways to join the cliff-top access track to Worms Head.

➤ Turn **left** along the firm, stony track, towards gates by the information centre.

1 ➤ Continue through the gate.

➤ Where track turns left by a drystone wall keep **straight on** along a wide grassy way.

☆ Dylan Thomas

Dylan Thomas, the Welsh poet famed for *Under Milk Wood*, was forced to spend the night on Worms Head after being caught out by the tides. He was intrigued by the dramatic, foreboding landscapes of Rhossili and, in letters to fellow poet and lover Pamela Hansord, he described the Worm as 'the very promontory of depression' and the long grasses he walked across as 'abominable' and like 'the long hairs of rats'.

☆ **The Vile** In medieval times land was often divided into narrow strips separated by earth banks. Most were ploughed up to allow modern mechanised farming methods but the National Trust has been restoring the fields of the Vile, between Rhossili and the coast. They grow around 400,000 sunflowers, which provide quite a splash of golden yellow in August and September. The restored field boundaries offer important corridors across the farmland for small mammals and invertebrates and create a haven for wildlife, including nesting birds.

Lookout Station, Worms Head

The Vile
☆ (left)

1 mile

Tears Point

2 ➤ Pass to **right** of Lookout Station then turn **left** along clifftop path.
➤ This meets a drystone wall and rounds the rim of a small inlet.
➤ Ignore gate at the top; continue along path, wall on left, to next headland.

3 ➤ Turn sharp **left** with the wall as the path looks down on Fall Bay.
➤ At the far end of Fall Bay, climb **left** beneath some rocks to wooden gate above a few steps.

NATURE NOTES

Skylarks frequent the area and choughs have recolonised the cliffs after an absence of over a century. Butterflies such as the small blue, gatekeeper and dark green fritillary can be seen fluttering over the fields and by the hedgerows. On the coast you may see Atlantic grey seals and common seals basking on the rocks (do not disturb them). The grey seal can be distinguished from the common seal as it is larger and has much coarser blotches on its brown/grey skin. Common seals have distinct V-shaped nostrils, while grey seals' nostrils are spaced apart. Noisy black and white guillemots and razorbills are often seen on the cliffs or feeding on the shoreline.

Top: grey seal
Above: common seal
Right: skylark

F a l l   B a y

1½ miles

4

2 miles

4 ➡ Go through gate and take the **right** fork across a field. ➡ Shortly after, climb steps to another gate. Go through and turn **left** to follow boundary to field corner in about 300 yards.

5 ➡ Jink **right** then immediately **left** with field-edge path, soon continuing on a fenced farm track to next path junction.

Guillemots

Dark green fritillary

Small blue

Gatekeeper

Middleton (right)

6 **7**

St Mary's Church
(right) ✝

2½ miles ı R h o s s i l i 🅿

National
Trust
car
park

6 ➡ Here, as track approaches the farms and houses of Middleton, double back **left** on another track.
➡ In about 200 yards meet a path junction, after the way becomes narrower and confined by hedgerows.

7 ➡ Turn **right** on a wide farm track, which takes the route back to the road in Rhossili.
➡ Go **left** along road back to car park.

This page (clockwise): The promenade at Mumbles; Broughton Beach; Dylan Thomas at Pump House, Swansea; Margam Abbey
Opposite (clockwise): Afan river; toposcope, Cefn Bryn; Pontrhydyfen

WALK 3

CEFN BRYN AND ARTHUR'S STONE

Known as the backbone of Gower, Cefn Bryn is the second highest peak on the peninsula after Rhossili Down. It offers wonderful, wide-sweeping views of the north and south coasts of the Gower. Ancient history is everywhere, including cairns and cromlechs, castles and historic trackways. All the height gain is achieved by your car in getting to the walk start! See from on high the secret coves and bays of south Gower and scan the vast salt marshes of the north, beyond which lie the pale blue haze of the Carmarthenshire hills.

Did you know? The ridge track along Cefn Bryn is known as Talbot's Road, named after the Mansel Talbot family who often drove their hounds along it after a hunt in Green Cwm and Parc le Breos.

28   Short Walks Made Easy

Local legend While on his way to Camlan, King Arthur is said to have thrown a stone across the Loughor Estuary. The stone grew in size as it flew over the waters and landed on Cefn Bryn. From that day the stone gained magic qualities and sometimes it creeps away to take a drink from the estuary.

OS information

🧭 SS 490900
Explorer 164

Distance
5 miles/8km

Time
3 hours

Start/Finish
Ridgetop car park above Reynoldston

Parking SA3 1AG
Roadside car park, about ½ mile east of Reynoldston

Public toilets
None

Cafés/pubs
Nearest, King Arthur Hotel, Reynoldston

Terrain
Firm grass paths and tracks

Hilliness
Gently undulating ridgetop

Footwear
Year round 👢

📷 **Public transport**
Bus service 118 from Swansea stops in Reynoldston, ½ mile from 🧭: traveline. cymru

♿ **Accessibility**
Suitable for all-terrain wheelchairs and pushchairs in dry conditions

🐕 **Dogs**
Welcome but keep on leads due to livestock and ponies. No stiles

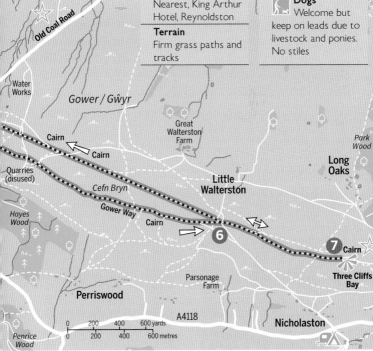

STORIES BEHIND THE WALK

☆ **Ancient cairns** Cefn Bryn is also scattered with prehistoric hut circles, burnt mounds and cairns, mostly from the Bronze Age, when it is believed that the ridge was used for ceremonies and rituals.

The Great Cairn, which lies close to Arthur's Stone, is the most prominent of these. It's a flattish cairn of around 65 feet in diameter. The acidic soils of Cefn Bryn meant that there were only traces of bones left in the chamber below but Mesolithic flints and remnants of Neolithic pottery were also discovered here.

☆ **The Old Coal Road** The tarred road that straddles the moor between Reynoldston and Cillibion is known as the Old Coal Road or the Red Road. The latter name comes from the colour of the old red sandstone which used to make up the road's surface. Coal was transported in carts from the coalfields of Pen-clawdd in northern Gower to the south coast of the peninsula.

Old Coal Road — Great Cairn ① ② — ③ Arthur's Stone · ½ mile — ④ Old Coal Road · 1 mile

➠ With the car park and road behind you, step **forward** onto a wide grassy swathe that turns into a clear path.
➠ Continue for about 200 yards to a fork.

① ➠ Branch **left** onto a slightly narrower grass path. This soon comes to the Great cairn.

Penrice Castle

Look southwards from the ridge towards Oxwich Bay and you might pick out the ruined ramparts of Penrice Castle, surrounded by woodland. The lands were given to the de Penrice family for their support in the Norman invasion. They built the stone castle in the 13th century. The last of the family, Isabel de Penrice, married Sir Hugh Mansel, who also bought Margam Abbey. The castle was damaged during the English Civil War. Thomas Mansel Talbot built a fine mansion in the grounds in the mid-1770s, now classified as a Grade I-listed building.

☆ Arthur's Stone

Arthur's Stone (Maen Ceti) is a Neolithic cromlech built as a communal burial ground. The capping stone weighs 25 tons. Henry VII detoured to the site on his way to the Battle of Bosworth Field. It was later discovered that the stone wasn't transported here at all, but was an erratic boulder deposited by a retreating ice sheet. The burial ground was created by digging beneath the stone and placing 12 additional stones to support it.

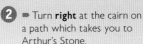

First summit ⏶ ⎹ 2 miles   Second summit ⏶

⎹ 1½ miles

Gower Way

View to the south to Penrice Castle, toposcope

2 ➠ Turn **right** at the cairn on a path which takes you to Arthur's Stone.

3 ➠ Pass to the **right** of the stone and continue on a clear, grass path gradually arcing **right** to return to road 200 yards from car park.
➠ Turn **right** on a roadside path to car park.

NATURE NOTES

The old red sandstone of the ridge protrudes from the surrounding beds of limestone supporting grasslands partially cloaked with bracken and western gorse, and interspersed with heathers and with cotton grass in the wetter areas. The marsh fritillary butterfly can be found here, fluttering over and pollinating the vegetation. Devil's-bit scabious is particularly important to the larvae of this species, both for feeding and hibernation.

At dusk you might be lucky enough to see a brown hare – it's bigger than a rabbit and has longer legs and long black-tipped ears.

Wild hill ponies roam the moors freely. For most of their young lives they are left to their own devices but when they reach adulthood they are often taken off the moor and sold.

Devil's-bit scabious

Third summit

Cairn and view to Three Cliffs Bay

7

3 miles

2½ miles

G o w e r   W a y

3½ miles

4 ➟ Path to Cefn Bryn lies across the road, marked by two boulders and a footpath signpost.
➟ Follow wide track along spine of the ridge (not the fainter one to the right) for ¼ mile to a view indicator.

5 ➟ Maintain direction past the toposcope (and stone seat) and continue along ridge, gently rising over the first two grassy summits of Cefn Bryn.
➟ 350 yards beyond the second summit, reach a track junction – note Gower Way marker for return.

Above: wild ponies
Below: bracken with foxgloves

Top: gorse with heather
Above: marsh fritillary

Old Coal Road ☆

| 4 miles | 4½ miles | 5 miles |

6 ➡ Carry on along ridge, passing **right** of the third and highest summit then keep going for about another 500 yards to the huge cairns overlooking Three Cliffs Bay.

7 ➡ Retrace your steps to the junction noted at **6**.
➡ Take **right** fork by Gower Way marker and water company grid.
➡ The arrow-straight track (ignore side paths) runs for 1.4 miles back to road.

8 ➡ On nearing road turn **left** along a parallel grass path to regain the start.

Walk 3 Cefn Bryn and Arthur's Stone   33

PENNARD CLIFFS AND PWLLDU HEAD

Pennard Cliffs are perhaps the most spectacular on Gower. This walk offers fantastic views of the cliffs and sands of Three Cliffs Bay, the attractive Pobbles Beach, the conical Shire Head and the great bulk of Pwlldu Head. Once the haunt of smugglers, this exhilarating cliff-top route has far-reaching views over the Bristol Channel to the uplands of Exmoor.

The route can be done as two separate walks, especially if you'd like more ice cream than walk! – one loop to Shire Head (**1** to **4**); the other to Pwlldu (**5** to **8**).

Did you know? Bones of woolly mammoth, hyena and woolly rhinoceros were discovered in Minchin Hole, a huge cave located in a ravine in the cliffs beneath High Tor.

Local legend Pennard Castle was a powerful fortress, the base for a ruthless and bloodthirsty baron whose exploits in battle had earned him the hand of the Prince of Gwynedd's daughter. The baron and his new bride returned to the castle

celebrate the wedding.
A group of fairies could be
heard dancing and playing music
with their harps. Out of sheer
madness, the baron and his
men, now very drunk, went to
slay them but their swords did
no harm. The fairies magically
disappeared after declaring that
they would have their revenge.
Suddenly there was a great
storm and ferocious winds
whipped up the sands around
the castle, soon enveloping it
and burying all within.

OS information

🧭 SS 553873
Explorer 164

Distance
4.5 miles / 7.2 km

Time
2½ hours

Start/Finish
Southgate

Parking SA3 2DH
National Trust
Southgate car park,
East Cliff Road

Public toilets
None

Cafés/pubs
Three Cliffs Coffee
Shop and The
Lookout, cafés
adjacent to car park;
pub and restaurants
in Southgate

Terrain
Surfaced paths and
tracks

Hilliness
Gently undulating
with moderate rise/
descent to/from
Pwlldu Head **8**

Footwear
Year round

Public transport
Bus service 14
between Swansea
and Southgate:
traveline.cymru

Accessibility
Wheelchairs on
lanes either side
of car park: West
Cliff (🧭 to **1**, and
parallel alternative
route to lane end –
over ½ mile there
and back) and East
Cliff (staying on lane
at **5** to **6** – over
1½ miles there and
back)

Dogs
Welcome.
No stiles

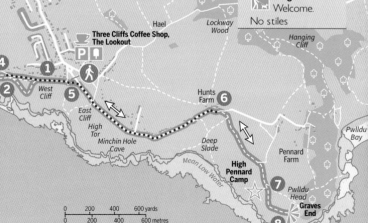

Southgate

Hael

Lockway Wood

Three Cliffs Coffee Shop, The Lookout

Hanging Cliff

4

1

2

West Cliff

5

East Cliff

High Tor

Minchin Hole Cave

Hunts Farm **6**

Deep Slade

Mean Low Water

High Pennard Camp

7

Pwlldu Head

Graves End

8

Pennard Farm

Pwlldu Bay

0 200 400 600 yards
0 200 400 600 metres

STORIES BEHIND THE WALK

☆ **Smugglers at Pwlldu** There are just a few cottages at Pwlldu (black pool) Beach these days but at one time it was a small port, exporting limestone from local quarries. There were two inns at that time – The Ship and The Beaufort. Names like Brandy Cove give a clue to the illicit goings on around the coast of Gower. Pwlldu's natural harbour made it an ideal place for smugglers. The Beaufort Inn still exists, but as a private house overlooking the bay.

☆ **Pennard Castle**

This was first built in the early 12th century by Henry Beaumont, the 1st Earl of Warwick, after he defeated the Welsh troops of Gower. A century later the castle and the title Lord of Gower passed to the de Braose family. They replaced the timber castle with a stone-built structure. A church and small settlement were built next to the castle at this time. Ownership of the castle changed several times but by the 16th century it was decaying and being overrun by the shifting sand dunes. Castle, church and village were abandoned.

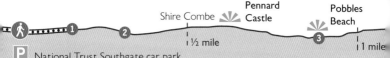

Shire Combe • Pennard ☆ Castle • Pobbles ☆ Beach

1½ mile ⋅ 1 mile

🅿 National Trust Southgate car park

☕ 📖 Three Cliffs Coffee Shop; The Lookout

➥ Go to the seaward end of the car park and turn **right** along the lane for 150 yards, watching out for a path marked by three boulders on the left.

1 ➥ Branch **left** on a clear grassy path between bushes.
➥ Gently rise to the headland of West Cliff, there going **right** along the cliff-line for about 100 yards back towards the lane.

☆ **High Pennard Camp** The Iron Age fort of High Pennard Camp is one of many along the Gower coast. It commands an impregnable position on the tall cliffs of Pwlldu Head. You may be able to pick out the low mounds and ditches that are partly concealed by gorse. The fort was excavated by Audrey Williams in 1939. The digs unearthed animal bones, shells, two sling stones and fragments of pottery dating back to the Romans.

☆ **Graves End**

On Pwlldu Head **8** you are standing above Graves End. The name is testament to a sad story. In 1760 a navy vessel, the *Caesar*, was shipwrecked. This was no ordinary ship but one commissioned to press-gang unwilling civilians into joining the Navy. Being locked below deck, many of those press-ganged died. They are buried in a mass grave under the cliff.

National Trust car park;
Three Cliffs Coffee Shop;
The Lookout

High Tor, Minchin Hole
Cave in cliffs below

4 1½ mile

5 P ☕ 🏪

▲ 2 miles

2 ▪ Just before road, bear **left** on wide bridleway that parallels the lane.
▪ After 200 yards, fork **left** on grassland path to cliffs above Shire Combe.
▪ Follow cliff-line **right** for about ⅓ mile to re-meet bridleway at wide junction.

3 ▪ There's a bench with a fine view 100 yards further along if you'd like a rest.
▪ Otherwise, double back **right** on a path crowded by bushes; it soon widens out.
▪ Keep to path for ½ mile to meet lane.

NATURE NOTES

The limestone geology of the area supports alpine plants such as yellow whitlow grass. Other coastal specialities to look out for are goldilocks aster and sea lavender. The coast path weaves through bramble and western gorse. Wild primroses can also be found in the shadier places.

Keep a lookout for common lizards basking on rocks or sandy ground along path edges. In high summer, dark green fritillary butterflies are on the wing. For a butterfly they are comparatively powerful, rapid flyers and enjoy open, sunny areas.

Choughs, ravens and peregrine falcons are masters of the skies. Peregrines are large powerful raptors and, after a decline in the 20th century, their numbers are now recovering and they're not an uncommon sight in Gower.

Above: yellow whitlow grass
Below: chough

Pwlldu Head and Graves End

High Pennard Camp (right) ☆

High Pennard Camp (left) ☆

7

8

Hunts Farm

6

3 miles

2½ miles

5 ➡ **Cross** car park and maintain direction on (East Cliff) lane.
➡ Past last of the parking bear **right** to use a parallel grass path.
➡ Path returns to lane near the last of the bungalows. Follow it to Hunts Farm.

4 ➡ Bear **right** onto lane and follow it all the way back to car park.

Peregrine falcon

Above: goldilocks aster
Below: sea lavender

½ miles   Hunts Farm   4 miles   4½ miles

6 ➥ Fork **right** on signposted path to Pwlldu (narrow at first with a very awkward pinch point for pushchairs).
➥ Follow coast path signs as path veers right to reach a junction below Iron Age hillfort (right).

7 ➥ Take **right** fork on path which passes to left of hillfort to reach the summit at Pwlldu Head.

National Trust Southgate car park 🅿
Three Cliffs Coffee Shop; ☕ ⛽
The Lookout

8 ➥ For the return, retrace your steps from Pwlldu Head to Hunts Farm via the outward route, and then follow the lane back to Southgate.

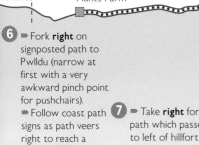

Opposite (clockwise): rock
pool; gannet; Japanese larch; birds
roosting at Whiteford Lighthouse
This page (clockwise):
meadow pipit; wild primroses;
wild pony above Rhossili Beach;
bluebells at Margam

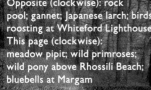

LANGLAND TO OYSTERMOUTH CASTLE

From the splendid cove of Langland Bay, a mainly tarred path squeezes its way between the gorse- and bracken-covered slopes of the headland and the rugged foreshore. It comes to the promontories of Mumbles, with its lighthouse, lifeboat station, popular pier and busy cafés, and then offers you a wide-sweeping view of Swansea Bay, all the way to the distant shores of Ogmore. Throughout the walk you are never far from a café, ice cream parlour or a pub to keep you refreshed.

Did you know? Oystermouth gets its name from its association with the oyster industry that thrived in the village until the 19th century. Unfortunately, pollution building up since the start of the Industrial Revolution finished the oyster fishery.

Local legend A lady in a long white dress has been seen in the grounds of Oystermouth Castle. Many believe her to be Alina de Breos, the last in the

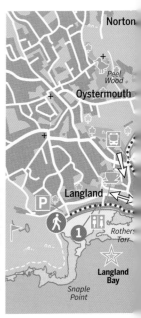

line of the powerful de Breos family, Lords of Gower. She married John de Mowbray in 1298. On her father's death an inconclusive will meant that Alina and John had to fight to regain control of the estate. John seized the castle but he was killed in a battle against King Edward II. Alina was then imprisoned in the Tower of London and had to wait until the monarch's death to return.

OS information

🚶 SS 605873
Explorer 164

Distance
3.5 miles/5.6 km (plus
½ mile bus ride and a
further ½ mile walk if
completing the circuit)

Time
2 hours (full circuit
2½ hours)

Start Langland Bay
Finish Oystermouth
Castle (to complete
circuit, take bus to
Langland Corner then
½ mile walk to 🚶)

Parking SA3 4SQ
Langland Bay car park

Public toilets
In car park; by
Mumbles Pier

Cafés/pubs
Langland Bay;
Mumbles;
Oystermouth

Terrain
Surfaced paths and
tracks

Hilliness
Steady gradient
along Newton Road,
Oystermouth

Footwear
Year round 👟

🚌 **Public transport**
Bus services
2, 2a, 2b run from
outside Marks and
Spencer on Newton
Road, Oystermouth,
to Langland Corner (a
½ mile downhill stroll
to car park): traveline.
cymru

♿ **Accessibility**
••••••••••
Suitable for all-terrain
wheelchairs and
pushchairs throughout

🐕 **Dogs**
Welcome but
keep on leads from
Mumbles Pier onwards
due to shared-use cycle
path. No stiles

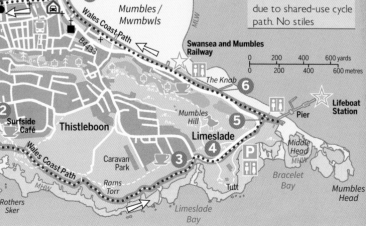

STORIES BEHIND THE WALK

☆ **Langland Bay** The small but lovely rocky cove, fine sands and its proximity to the towns of the Swansea Bay area made Langland Bay a popular resort in Victorian times, and more so in the 1950s and 60s, when there were fine hotels. Many have now been turned into apartments. The resort is known for its long rows of colourful beach huts.

☆ Lifeboats and disaster

There has been a lifeboat station in Mumbles since 1866. The newest of the stations lies at the end of Mumbles Pier with an older slipway adjacent to it. Tragedy struck in 1947 when all eight crew of the lifeboat drowned in the attempted rescue of the *SS Samtampa* which had run aground at Sker Point, Porthcawl.

Langland Bay ☆

Surfside Café; Rotherslade Bay ☕

½ mile

1 mile

P Langland Bay car park

🚻 ☕

1 ➤ Turn **right** immediately beyond the toilets then **left** along the promenade, which climbs slightly and descends gently to Rotherslade Bay and the Surfside Café.

➤ Facing towards the sea, go **left** across the car park behind the beach huts to reach the toilet block.

2 ➤ Pass the café either by the stairs or the ramps and continue on a tarred coastal path for slightly over 1 mile to a road end at Limeslade Bay.

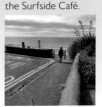

☆ Swansea and Mumbles Railway

The need to transport coal, limestone and iron-ore efficiently to Swansea's docks was the catalyst for building the railway-cum-tramway. Opened in 1807 as a horse-drawn tramway linking the Swansea Canal with Castle Hill, Oystermouth, it soon carried the world's first fare-paying railway passengers along the bay. Steam trains first operated in 1877 and the line was extended to Mumbles Pier in 1898. In 1928 it became electrified but the line finally closed in 1960. The front of one of the electric trams (No 7) can be seen in the National Waterfront Museum, Swansea.

🏰 Oystermouth Castle

In 1106, after conquering Gower, the Normans built Oystermouth Castle on a strategically sited limestone ridge overlooking Swansea Bay. But these were turbulent times and wars with the Welsh resulted in the castle being taken several times over the next 300 years. In 1203 the lordship of Gower and Oystermouth Castle was granted to William de Breos. He made extensive additions to the castle, though by the mid-17th century it had become ruinous. However, in 2009 the National Assembly for Wales refurbished the castle and opened it to the public.

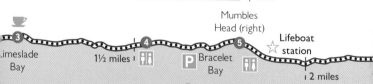

Mumbles Head (right)

Lifeboat station

Limeslade Bay

1½ miles

P Bracelet Bay

2 miles

4 ➡ Go through car park entrance and turn **left**.
➡ Keep **forward**, parallel to road, through successive car parks. By the final car park the road makes a marked left-hand bend.

3 ➡ Follow the coast road to the Bracelet Bay car parks.

NATURE NOTES

Langland Bay is a Site of Importance for Nature Conservation (SINC). Short-beaked dolphins, harbour porpoise and shoals of sand eels are found here. The last-mentioned are a very important part of the food chain for seabirds. The sand eel will bury itself in seabed sediment to escape predation, hence its name. Exploring the sea-eroded, carboniferous limestone rock pools at low tide you may find common prawn, shanny (a type of blenny), butterfish (small eel), tiny stalked jellyfish and snakelocks anemone. Be careful with this anemone as its wavy tentacles can give you a nasty sting.

Gannets can also be seen plunging into the sea for fish, and Mumbles Pier is a good place to spot kittiwakes.

Bright yellow ragwort adds colour to the grass banks above Bracelet Bay. It's hated by farmers as it's poisonous to both cattle and horses but it is a valuable pollinator and is of significant ecological importance.

Above: kittiwake

Oystermouth Castle

☆ Swansea and Mumbles Railway

2½ miles

3 miles

5 ➤ Ignore bend and keep **right** on No Entry tarred lane, curving and descending fairly steeply to Mumbles Pier.
➤ Turn **left** by pier and follow the coastal drive/promenade to a wall gap in about 450 yards.

6 ➤ Turn through the gap and then go **left** past the local yacht club's boat park.
➤ Continue for ¾ mile along promenade past cafés and bars to car park toilet block and pay station.

Ragwort at Bracelet Bay

Snakelocks anemone

Sand eel

3½ miles

Langland Corner

Surfside Café

4 miles

Langland Bay car park

7 ➠ Angle **left** to use tarred path under trees to main road.
➠ Cross over and rise along Newton Road ahead.
➠ Just beyond M&S Food, turn **right** on Castle Road, then first **right** through gate onto tarred track to Oystermouth Castle.

8 ➠ Turn up **left** to visit castle.
➠ Return to M&S for bus stop and catch the 2, 2a, 2b bus to Langland Corner.
➠ Alighting from bus, take Rotherslade Road (middle one of three) to **left**. This descends to **2** where you turn **right** back to the start.

SWANSEA
HERITAGE WALK

Wales' second city (after Cardiff), Swansea is a rejuvenated and vibrant place as this walk reveals. Setting out along the promenade, it then accompanies the River Tawe past the marinas with their colourful yachts and harbourside cafés. The Tawe is crossed and re-crossed on two modern bridges before you head for the historic Maritime Quarter and its fascinating and varied museums. You'll discover the city's Norman castle before returning via the shopping centre back to the promenade.

OS information	
🚶 SS 653924 Explorer 165	
Distance 2.9 miles/4.6km	
Time 1½ hours	
Start/Finish Paxton Street car park, Swansea	
Parking SA1 3SA Paxton Street car park	
Public toilets At the marina, near	
Cafés/pubs Swansea	
Terrain Pavement	
Hilliness Flat	
Footwear Year round	

Public transport

Swansea has a mainline railway station and is a hub for coach and bus services: traveline.cymru

Accessibility

Wheelchair and pushchair friendly throughout

Dogs
Welcome but keep on leads. No stiles

Did you know? Poet Dylan Thomas worked for the *South Wales Daily Post* at the newspaper's castle site in the early 1930s. It was his first job after leaving school and he worked as journalist on the paper for 18 months. In 1932 the paper's title changed to the *South Wales Evening Post*. In 1976 they moved their offices away from the castle site.

Local legend A man who committed suicide on the Helwick lightship is said to haunt the Swansea Museum. Apparently, he appears as a dark-hooded figure wandering up and down its staircase, while the vessel itself is one of the museum's floating exhibits.

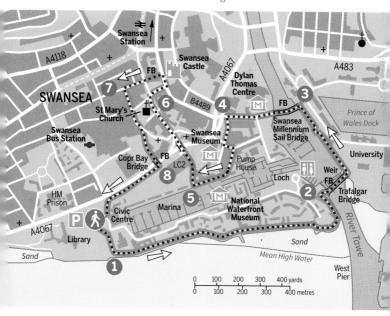

STORIES BEHIND THE WALK

☆ **History of Swansea** The name Swansea derives from the Norse 'Sweyn eh' after King Sweyn Forkbeard (960–1014), who used it as a trading post. The Normans conquered the area in the early 12th century, Swansea becoming the chief town in the Marcher Lordship of Gower.

From the early 18th century Swansea became the world's largest copper-smelting area. Smelting required large amounts of limestone and coal and, to meet those needs, tramways and railways were built along the supply routes. In the mid-19th century Swansea had 600 active furnaces. Visiting in 1860, John Murray wrote that the glare crossing Llandore Bridge at night brought to mind Dante's *Inferno*.

The 19th and 20th centuries saw the gradual decline of the copper and coal industries. During World War II, Swansea suffered the Three Nights' Blitz, which destroyed much of the town centre. Rebuilding from the 1950s is being replaced and modern marinas have transformed the old docks.

½ mile

P Paxton Street car park

W a t e r f r o n t   p r o m

➊ ➡ Take the tarred path to the promenade and turn **left** along it.
➡ Follow promenade for ¾ mile and turn **left** on meeting the River Tawe to reach Trafalgar Bridge.

➡ Walk through car park towards seafront, **cross** the road and follow the signed cycle path past another car park.

Swansea Castle

Swansea Castle was founded by Henry de Beaumont in 1106. Its history is inextricably linked with Oystermouth Castle, both being seats of the Lords of Gower. Like Oystermouth, it was overrun and destroyed several times by the Welsh, including defeats by Owain Glyndŵr and Llywelyn the Great. The ruins seen today are from the 13th and 14th century. In the 18th century it was used as a workhouse.

Swansea's museums

Swansea records its heritage well, particularly in the restored buildings and museums of the Maritime Quarter. The Dylan Thomas Centre, built in the former Guildhall, was restored in 1995 and was opened by ex-US President, Jimmy Carter.

Swansea Museum houses art galleries and its exhibits include vintage transport, fossil trees from Coelbren, and a glass-walled tramway centre on the marina's waterfront, while on the quayside are the floating exhibits.

The National Waterfront Museum celebrates Wales' industrial history, including modern technologies.

(125 yards)   Trafalgar Bridge and Weir

e n a d e   1 mile River Tawe   Swansea Millennium Sail Bridge

2 ➡ Double back **right** to the riverfront to **cross** Trafalgar Bridge.
➡ Turn **left** along the far bank and stroll to next bridge.

3 ➡ Turn **left** across Swansea Millennium Sail Bridge and go **straight on** along Somerset Place, passing the Dylan Thomas Centre, to junction with Adelaide Street.

Walk 6 Swansea Heritage Walk   **51**

NATURE NOTES

Harbour porpoise can be seen swimming offshore in Swansea Bay. These protected mammals are quite small compared to their cousins, the dolphins. They have a high metabolic rate in the cool coastal waters surrounding Britain and need to eat enough fish to replenish as much as 10 per cent of their own body weight each day.

Trafalgar Bridge (after ②) is a likely spot to watch cormorants peering over the weir. These large, long-necked black birds are excellent divers and very proficient at catching fish.

The sands are a fine place to go beachcombing. Look for the shells of common whelks, mussels, cockles and scallops, which have been washed up on the tides. The pink and white-flowered sea bindweed grows on the beach-edge sands.

Above: cormorant

1½ miles

| Dylan Thomas Centre | Swansea Museum (right) | Waterfront Museum | St Mary's Church (left) |

Marina & Pump House

LCL2 (left); Museum Green (right)

2 miles

④ ➡ Go **left** on Adelaide Street. At Swansea Museum turn **left** along Cambrian Place then first **right** into Gloucester Place, passing Seamen's Church.
➡ Just beyond it, turn **right** past the red-bricked Pump House. Follow the harbourside to far end of National Waterfront Museum.

⑤ ➡ Turn **right**, following paved path keeping to right-hand side of LC2 Building and along left side of Museum Green.
➡ Use pedestrian crossing over dual carriageway.
➡ Go **straight on** up Princess Way, passing Travelodge and St Mary's Church to mini-roundabout.

⑥ ➡ Turn **right** to reach the square and the castle.
➡ Walk **anti-clockwise** round three sides of the square then cross Princess Way and keep ahead along main shopping precinct to junction opposite Marks and Spencer.

Harbour porpoise

Top: pink sea bindweed
Above: shells

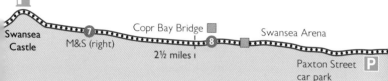
Swansea Castle

7 M&S (right)

Copr Bay Bridge

8

2½ miles

Swansea Arena

Paxton Street car park

7 ▬ Turn **left** down Oxford Street.
▬ Where this bends left, leave it by keeping **ahead** along Cupid Way, which leads to a dazzling bridge.

8 ▬ Go over Copr Bay Bridge then turn **right** in front of Swansea Arena and follow pedestrianised walkway back to car park.

AFAN FOREST PARK

The Afan Valley is typical of many in South Wales in that, after 200 years of heavy industry, it has been returned to countryside. Forests have replaced slag heaps and pit winding wheels. This walk uses old railway and tramway trackbeds for pleasant strolls through the trees. Colourful wildflowers deck the verges while the Afon (river) Afan flows through the valley below, crystal clear. Salmon and trout swim up the river these days!

Halfway round there's a visitor centre, café and the fascinating South Wales Miners' Museum.

OS information
⊗ SS 799941 Explorer 165
Distance 3.6 miles/5.8km
Time 2 hours
Start/Finish Afan Forest Park
Parking SA12 9SG Rhyslyn car park, Afan Forest Park, Pontrhydyfen
Public toilets At visitor centre, during opening hours
Cafés/pubs Café at visitor centre; Miners Arms, Pontrhydyfen
Terrain Surfaced paths and tracks

Did you know? Pontrhydyfen's town sign
says it is the birthplace of the great film actor
Richard Burton, the Broadway musical star Ivor
Emmanuel and the opera singer Rebecca Evans.
While two of the claims are true, Ivor Emmanuel
(the author's uncle) was actually born in Margam.
However, he did spend most of his childhood in
the village and was a friend of Richard Burton.

Local legend The King of the Hill, disguised as
a goblin, came across a young girl called Elen,
somewhere in the Afan Valley. He promised her
all the treasures she desired from his kingdom
as long as she didn't tell a soul what she'd seen.
Elen took the treasures but didn't keep her
promise. The treasures vanished and she never
laid eyes on the king again.

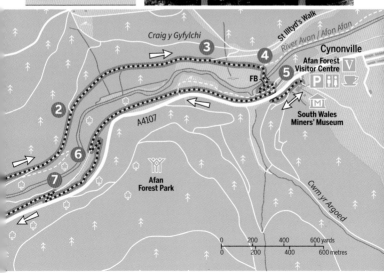

STORIES BEHIND THE WALK

☆ Rhondda and Swansea Bay Railway

The walk begins close to the site of the former railway station while the return leg utilises the trackbed of the old Rhondda and Swansea Bay Railway. It fully opened in 1895 and joined Swansea with Treherbert in the Rhondda Valley, with links to Port Talbot and Briton Ferry. The line included a steep climb out of Treherbert to reach the Rhondda Tunnel. At nearly 2 miles, it was the longest in Wales. In 1968 the Rhondda Tunnel collapsed and now only a short section of the line around Briton Ferry and Swansea is in use.

Treherbert station

☆ Industry in the Afan Valley

Until the early 19th century, land use in the steep-sided Afan Valley was mainly agricultural. John Reynolds started a huge ironworks in Pontrhydyfen in 1824, with two blast furnaces. He built a 2-mile watercourse to supply power via a water wheel, which meant constructing a four-arched viaduct, Bont Fawr, to carry the water over

Pontrhydyfen, birthplace of Richard Burton (500 yards)

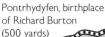

Rhyslyn car park

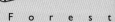
A f a n   F o r e s t

➤ From the far end of Rhyslyn car park take the **leftmost** of two tracks heading into the forest.

① ➤ Pass through the barrier. A radar key is required to open the disabled access gate.
➤ Follow the gently rising, stony forest road for almost ¾ mile to a main fork, with the Afon Afan (river) down below on the right.

the Afan. He also built a tramway to Aberafon, near Port Talbot, to export the iron. The works were sold in 1838 and by the late 19th century production had ceased.

Coal pits proliferated here in the late 19th century, as did the tramways and railways that served them. But by the 1960s the industry had dwindled and the pits were closed. Find out more at the South Wales Miners' Museum.

The Afan Forest The forests of the Afan Valley were first planted by the Forestry Commission between the 1930s and 1950s as part of a national timber supply scheme. The timber had been needed locally for pit-props. As the coal mines were closed and the hillsides re-landscaped, more plantations of spruce, pine and larch were added and today they cover large swathes of the valley and uplands. Designated as a Forest Park in 1972, the area was developed for cycling and walking, repurposing the old railways, miners' tracks and tramways.

ı 1 mile

Bridge over
Afon Afan

P a r k

ı 1½ miles

2 ➡ Take the lower (**right**) fork and stroll for just over ½ mile to the next main forest track junction.

3 ➡ Again take the **right** fork, descending towards the river to a path junction in the valley bottom.

NATURE NOTES

Although the forest is mainly coniferous, once the trees are mature and have been harvested they are gradually being replaced by broadleaved trees such as oak, alder, birch and sycamore. On the lower slopes of the valley you'll be able to spot Japanese larch, which, unlike other conifers, drops its needles in winter. Scots and Corsican pines thrive on the drier mid-slopes while on the upper slopes you'll see the darker hues of Sitka spruce, a most resilient and fast-growing tree.

There are plenty of bluebells, foxgloves and red campions growing along the verges of the tracks in spring and summer.

All three native woodpeckers may be found in Afan Forest.

The largest is the colourful green woodpecker but, mainly feeding on ants, it spends more time on the ground than in the trees. The great spotted woodpecker has boldly marked black and white plumage. Listen out for its tapping or drumming as its chisel-shaped bill hammers into decaying tree trunks. The lesser spotted woodpecker is the scarcest and shyest. Little bigger than a sparrow it generally stays high up in the trees.

Green woodpecker

V Afan Forest Visitor Centre; Miners' Museum

P M

2 miles

Afan

2½ miles

Old railway trackbed

4 ➡ Swing **right** to cross the wooden footbridge and take the stony walkers' path, which **zigzags uphill** to an old railway trackbed, emerging in front of a flyover.

5 ➡ The walk continues **right** along the trackbed for ¾ mile to its abrupt end.
➡ But first, to visit the café or Miners' Museum, go under bridge ahead and swing **left**. Return under bridge and go **left** to resume.

Above: foxglove
Below: bluebells

Great spotted woodpecker

Left: Lesser spotted woodpecker

F o r e s t   P a r k

Pontrhydyfen, birthplace of Richard Burton (500 yards)
Bridge over Afon Afan

3 miles

Old railway trackbed
3½ miles

Rhyslyr car park

6 ➡ At the end of the trackbed follow the tarred path which **zigzags uphill** and continues on a higher level until it **zigzags downhill** to rejoin the original trackbed in almost ½ mile.

7 ➡ Go **left** along the trackbed to a steel-railed bridge over the river.

8 ➡ **Cross** the bridge to return to the car park.

Opposite (clockwise):
Surfside Café,
Langland Bay; The
River House in the old
ice house, Swansea
This page (clockwise):
The Coast Café,
Swansea; Forte's
Ice Cream Parlour,
Limeslade; Welsh
cakes; The Lookout,
Rhossili; Coffee cart,
Ogmore Bay

WALK 8

CATCH A BUS

MARGAM

COUNTRY PARK

This magnificent country park is sited on grassy pastures beneath low, afforested hills, and is full of history and adventure. There's an old Cistercian abbey and an even older Iron Age fort on a hill overlooking a fairytale castle. You'll find a café, places for children to play, deer grazing on open pastures and a farm trail, where you can see a herd of rare Glamorgan cattle. There are also a couple of lakes for viewing wildfowl and you may even spot the odd pike!

OS information

🚶 SS 800860
Explorer 165

Distance
2.6 miles/4.2km

Time
1½ hours

Start/Finish
Margam Country Park

Parking SA13 2TJ
Margam Country Park car park

Public toilets
In car park; by café at Margam Castle

Cafés/pubs
Charlotte's Pantry café by the castle

Terrain
Surfaced paths and tracks

Hilliness
Mostly level; gentle rise at 🚶 and gentle descent at the end

Footwear
Year round 👢

Public transport
Bus service X1 between Swansea and Bridgend stops by the entrance to the park: traveline. cymru

Accessibility ♿ ▪▪▪▪▪▪▪▪▪▪
Wheelchair and pushchair friendly throughout using alternative route to avoid steps ⑦ to ⑧

Dogs Prohibited between ③ and ④; on leads elsewhere. No stiles

Did you know? In World War II, Margam Castle was used by both British and US troops. General Dwight Eisenhower, later to be US President, visited during preparations for the D-Day landings.

Local legend On the morning of 10 June 1898 the body of Robert Scott, Margam's gamekeeper, was found. He had been shot while looking for a man in dark clothing who had been seen poaching in the woods. It is said that the ghost of Scott can be seen on the stairs of the castle and is known for throwing stones at anyone trying to pursue him.

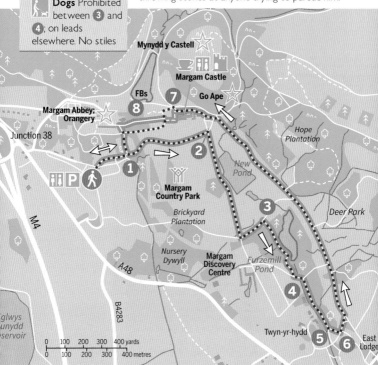

STORIES BEHIND THE WALK

☆ **Early History of the Margam Estate** The estate was first occupied in the Iron Age when Mynydd y Castell (Castle Mountain) fort was established on a hill that now overlooks the castle. After the Norman invasion of Wales, the estate lands were granted by Robert, 1st Earl of Gloucester, to the Cistercians of Clairvaux

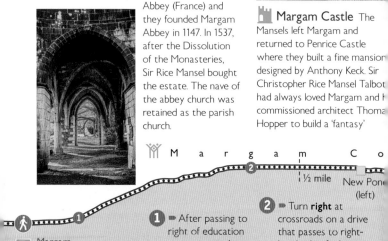

Abbey (France) and they founded Margam Abbey in 1147. In 1537, after the Dissolution of the Monasteries, Sir Rice Mansel bought the estate. The nave of the abbey church was retained as the parish church.

🏰 **Margam Castle** The Mansels left Margam and returned to Penrice Castle where they built a fine mansion designed by Anthony Keck. Sir Christopher Rice Mansel Talbot had always loved Margam and h commissioned architect Thoma Hopper to build a 'fantasy'

Margam C o

½ mile New Pon (left)

P Margam Country Park
🚻 car park

➡ From the car park, go through the park gates and pay kiosk.

1 ➡ After passing to right of education centre car park, veer **right** on tarred drive which heads for the castle but passes on its right-hand side and leads to a crossroads.

2 ➡ Turn **right** at crossroads on a drive that passes to right-hand side of a large pond and left of a children's playground.
➡ Turn **left** at next crossroads to T-junction in 150 yards.

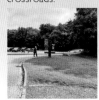

The Country Park

The Mansel Talbot family continued to use Margam as their home until 1941. It was sold to David Bevan a year later. Bevan never lived in the castle and it gradually fell into disrepair. Glamorgan County Council bought it in 1973. In 1977 a terrible fire gutted the interior of the castle. This was the catalyst for an ambitious restoration project. The 850-acre estate was developed into a wonderful country park with beautifully manicured gardens around the castle and orangery, expansive lawn-like pastures, children's playgrounds, and woodlands and lakes for wildlife.

astle in Tudor Gothic style, one
hat highlighted his position and
ortunes. By 1836 Hopper had
ven him the truly magnificent
astle seen today. It was built
sing sandstone from nearby Pyle.
he interior was just as opulent
nd was hung with paintings by
enowned artists such as Rubens.

u   n   t   r   y   P   a   r   k

Furzemill
Pond (left)

1 mile

Farm
buildings

 ➌ ➡ Go **right** on path through
tall gate where there's a 'no
dogs' sign.
➡ Pass another lake before
meeting a drive near a farm.
➡ Turn **left** and then keep
right on drive towards
farmhouse.

 ➍ ➡ Approaching farm
buildings fork **left** on a path
through woodland.
➡ Continue to another tall
gate at the far end of woods.

NATURE NOTES

Deer have been kept at Margam since the abbey was built. The monks were known to have kept hounds to hunt them. The current herd of 400 consists mainly of fallow deer, with some red deer and rare Père David's deer or milu, which originated in China. The park supports a wide range of birdlife. There's a flourishing population of skylarks and you may well see the colourful kingfisher around the streams. The adder, Britain's only poisonous snake, comes out from hibernation in the spring and might typically be seen basking on a rock in the sunshine.

On the lakes beyond the fringe of flag iris and yellow lilies are moorhens, coots, mallards, Canada geese, mute swans and that shyest and elusive of fish-eating mammals, the otter.

Buzzards may be seen soaring and kestrels hovering in the skies above Margam, patiently hunting for their prey.

Top: flag iris
Above: otters

Go Ape (right)

1½ miles

D e e r   P a r k
M a r g a m   C o u n t r y   P a r k

5 ➡ Turn **left** alongside a tall deer fence to reach a surfaced driveway with an enormous metal gate and huge kissing-gate.

6 ➡ Go **left** through it. Bend **left** with main drive in 75 yards and, ignoring side turnings, keep **forward** for ¾ mile to Go Ape.
➡ Curve **left** towards castle outbuildings (café, toilets); pass **right** of these to gates beyond oval green.

Above: kingfisher
Left: fallow deer

Castle
garden
entrance

Central broad
path with
terraced steps

🏰 **Margam**
Castle

┊ 2 miles ☕ 🚻 ⑦

Margam Abbey;
☆ **Orangery**

⑧

┊ 2½ miles

🅿️
🚻

Margam
Country
Park car
park

⑦ ➤ To avoid steps, use enclosed path/ramp **ahead**. Wind down, go **left** to cross central walkway then turn **right**, descending to undercroft.
➤ Otherwise, go **left** into formal garden. In a few strides take broad, central walkway on **right** with tiered steps through garden to last of the steps.

⑧ ➤ Pass octagonal ruin and double back **left** between undercroft and orangery to path junction. Alternative route rejoins here.
➤ Go through gates, keep to right-hand side of education centre car park and turn **right** through entrance gates.

Walk 8 Margam Country Park **67**

CATCH A BUS

PARC SLIP

This is a peaceful place created by the
Wildlife Trust, where the sights and
sounds of heavy industry have been
replaced with woodland and birdsong.
The nature walks here are easy, with
firm surfaced paths and tracks through
grassland, by streams, ponds and lakes,
and through shady woodland. Before
returning to the start you should have
seen birds galore, butterflies, flowers
and some fine wood sculptures. It's
a place you could come to again
and again to see the varying wildlife
through each season.

OS information	
🚶 SS 881841 Explorer 151	
Distance	1.9 miles/3.1km
Time	1 hour
Start/Finish	Parc Slip Nature Reserve
Parking CF32 0EH	Parc Slip Visitor Centre car park, Aberkenfig
Public toilets	At visitor centre
Cafés/pubs	Café at visitor centre (Apr–Oct, Wed–Sun); The Fountain pub
Terrain	Surfaced paths and tracks

Hilliness
One gentle climb near the end

Footwear
Year round 👢

🚌 Public transport
Bus service 63 between Bridgend and Porthcawl stops at The Fountain (pub) on B4281 (10-minute walk from 🚶): traveline.cymru

♿ Accessibility
••••••••••
Wheelchair and pushchair friendly throughout

🐕 Dogs
Welcome but keep on leads. No stiles

Did you know? The original village of Kenfig, probably founded by Robert, Earl of Gloucester, in the early 12th century, used to lie on the coast. Shifting sands were always a problem but storms during the 1300s made things worse and eventually led to the village being abandoned. John Leland, the English antiquarian, travelled through South Wales in 1539 and saw the ruins of old Kenfig village and its castle, both overrun with the sands 'that the Severn Sea casteth up'.

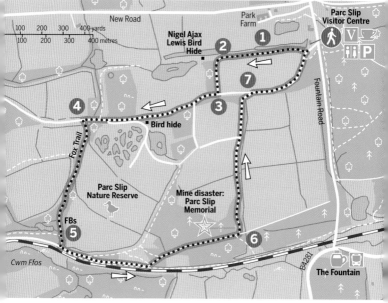

STORIES BEHIND THE WALK

☆ **Early History of the Mine** In 1864 a drift mine was opened by John Brogden and Sons for the extraction of house coal. At the height of its production the mine had two drifts. The main one was 4,000 feet long and mined eight seams. Although the geology was difficult, by the 1890s 200 men and boys were producing 300 tons of coal per day. The site wasn't known to be gaseous but locked safety lamps were mandatory.

☆ **The Mine Disaster** On 26 August 1892 the people of the area were looking forward to the annual Horse and Pleasure Fair on St Mary Hill. At 8.20am an explosion was heard, coming from the mine. Immediate rescue attempts were made but operations were hampered by roof collapses. The efforts lasted several days. Forty-two miners were brought out alive, but the final death toll was 112 men and boys. Investigations determined that the explosion was brought about by a hole in one of the miners' Davy lamps.

Bird hide (ahead)

Bird hide (ahead)

🦆 **Parc Slip Nature Reserve**

Parc Slip Visitor Centre

➡ From the car park, with your back to the road, go through small gate on the **right** by the visitor centre's bike racks. You will be following the Fox Trail.

① ➡ The path passes picnic benches, then pools and wetlands.
➡ Continue to next path junction.

Creation of the Nature Reserve After its closure in 1904, the stricken mine and its slag heaps lay waste for decades. However, in the 1960s the Parc Slip site was re-opened as an opencast mine and the landscape was once again transformed. It remained open for 30 years before the site was made safe and restored to agricultural and recreational land by the National Coal Board. With the help of the Glamorgan Wildlife Trust natural habitats were established. The site was handed over to the trust in 1999 and today is operated by the Wildlife Trust of South and West Wales. A visitor centre with a 3D-interactive exhibition and a café were built next to the car park, and information boards and sculptures were added around the site.

Stream and
small waterfalls

½ mile

2 ➡ Approaching the Nigel Ajax Lewis bird hide turn **left**.
➡ Stroll to next junction, passing a pond with nearby seat and then a statue of a coal miner and his son.

3 ➡ Turn **right** and follow Fox Trail to path junction in ⅓ mile. Watch for the Bittern Bird Hide along the way.

Walk 9 Parc Slip **71**

NATURE NOTES

Numerous species of orchid can be found in the fields and along the grass verges of the nature reserve's tracks. Among these are the early purple, bee, pyramidal, southern marsh and common spotted orchids.

In summer, besides the orchids, tall oxeye daisies and ragged robin add a superb carpet of colour in the open grassland. The fields also provide a habitat for skylark and lapwing. If you spot a small brown-streaked bird it will probably be the meadow pipit, which feeds on seeds and small insects in the meadow. Other frequent visitors include butterflies, such as the small tortoiseshell and red admiral, as well as the five-spot burnet moth.

In and around the ponds you may be lucky enough to spot the rare great crested newt, which looks like a tiny dragon. You're more likely to see dragonflies, including the common hawker.

Top: pit pony sculpture
Left: badger sculpture
Opposite: **top**, early purple orchid; **middle**, bee orchid; **bottom**, common spotted orchid

Mine disaster;
Parc Slip Memorial

 Parc Slip Nature Reserve ☆

⑥

1 mile

④ ➠ Turn **left**, waymarked Fox Trail, beside a stream with some pretty, if small, waterfalls to reach path junction in ¼ mile.

⑤ ➠ Go **left** in front of a tall blue National Cyclists Network sign.
➠ In ½ mile reach junction with blue fingerpost signed Parc Slip.

Above: small tortoiseshell butterfly
Below: red admiral butterfly

 1½ miles

 7

P
V
🚻
☕

🐦 Parc Slip Nature Reserve

6 ➧ Turn **left** and pause at the Parc Slip memorial.
➧ Climb gently for ⅓ mile, passing a side path (left) and going on to meet a track joining from the left.

Parc Slip
Visitor
Centre

7 ➧ Swing **right** to continue back to visitor centre.

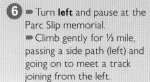

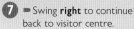

Walk 9 Parc Slip   **73**

OGMORE: COAST AND DOWNS

Ogmore is sited by the estuary of the river of the same name with an outlook to the great expanse of the Merthyr Mawr Warren. The walk towards Southerndown sustains great views from the low limestone cliffs out across the Bristol Channel to Exmoor. You can get refreshment at Southerndown before heading inland through the lovely rolling landscapes of Ogmore Down. The route takes you back to the river for a fine finale by the estuary and back to the beach.

OS information
SS 861755 Explorer 151
Distance 4.6 miles/7.4km
Time 2½ hours
Start/Finish Ogmore-by-Sea
Parking CF32 0QA Ogmore Beach car park
Public toilets In car park
Cafés/pubs Café at West Farm; Three Golden Cups pub, Southerndown
Terrain Generally firm paths through sandy grassland; lanes
Hilliness One short climb between ❷ and ❸; steady descent on Ogmore Down
Footwear Year round
Public transport Bus service 303 between Bridgend and Llantwit Major stops at Ogmore-by-Sea: traveline.cymru

Did you know? There are stories of smugglers deliberately causing shipwrecks for their personal gain by luring unsuspecting ships onto the rocks using false lights. Nobody was ever convicted.

Local legend There's a tale of a man who was woken from his sleep by a lady in a white dress. She beckoned him to follow her down to Ogmore Castle and, although he was reluctant at first, he went with her to the ruins of the old fortress. She showed him a chest full of gleaming gold coins and told him to help himself to what he needed, but no more. He became a rich man. But he grew greedy. One day, returning for more, the white lady refused him and said his good luck would now end. The rich man became sick and grew weaker. It is said that he died of Y Ladi Wen's (the white lady's) revenge.

Accessibility

Wheelchairs from ⓚ to ①; in dry conditions and with support and a robust, powered chair, as far as ②. All-terrain pushchairs throughout using alternative route ④ to ⑦ to avoid overgrowth and soft sand

Dogs

Welcome. No stiles

STORIES BEHIND THE WALK

☆ **Mari Flanders** After ❻ the route descends to a sandy, grass hollow known as Pant Mari Flanders – a pant is a clearing. Mari was a Flemish weaver, who like many from Flanders, came to Wales to escape religious persecution. She helped the locals trading wool from the sheep that roamed Ogmore Down. You'll pass Mari Flanders' Well, which was extremely important for both livestock and the locals before the days of mains water.

🏰 **Ogmore Castle**
A Norman baron, William de Londres, built the castle in the early years of the 12th century. The first castle would have been made from wood. The whole of Wales was an unfriendly place for the Normans and they

Wales Coast Path

Ogmore Beach (right) · ½ mile

Bristol Channel views and Tusker Rock

1 mile

Ogmore Beach car park
🚶 🅿 🚻

➡ With your back to the estuary, and keeping the sea on your right, follow tarmac lane past all the car parks and go through gate at the end to access waymarked coast path.

❶ ➡ Follow the coast path, mostly grass, alongside a drystone wall on left.
➡ Where the wall veers away left, keep **ahead** on coast path as signed.
➡ In ¾ mile arrive at a distinct rock-fringed hollow.

❷ ➡ Turn **inland**. The path climbs on a short rocky section followed by a grassy stretch to the road.

⚓ Shipwrecks

The coast off Ogmore and Porthcawl is renowned for its shipwrecks, with the notorious south-westerly winds running vessels onto the rocks. At low tide, you'll be able to see Tusker Rock, a dangerous reef about a mile or so out to sea. It hides just beneath the waves at high tide. The broken remains of several wrecks are visible at low tide.

One of the worst tragedies involved a Portuguese coal ship bound for Rio de Janeiro during a terrible storm in 1886. The vessel had lost its rudder and was drifting into shore. Communication lines were down and the Porthcawl lifeboat crew couldn't be contacted. Tragically, 20 sailors' lives were lost.

ere often attacked by Welsh
arlords. After one such skirmish
he castle was rebuilt in stone and
as occupied for a further 300
ears. Ownership passed to the
ouse of Lancaster, the monarchs
England. They had no need for
is outpost and, gradually, it fell
to ruin.

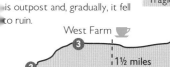

West Farm ☕
3
2
1½ miles
4
2 miles
5 Groes Farm

3 ➡ Turn **right** along the road.
➡ At West Farm café leave road and follow wall round back of café/farm complex then turn **left** to rejoin road.
➡ Follow this away from coast for 100 yards to path on left.

4 ➡ Go **left** and follow hedge-lined track to Groes Farm in ½ mile.
➡ Due to summer vegetation, pushchairs should follow road (pavement starts soon) into Southerndown, going **left** at crossroads to **5**, and keep forward on lane for 1⅓ miles, passing Norton, to **7**.

NATURE NOTES

The limestone rocks of the shoreline support the snail-like common dog whelks, limpets and winkles. The dog whelk feeds on mussels and barnacles. It drills through their shells and injects enzymes that dissolve the prey, and then sucks it out of the shell through its proboscis. You may see crabs in the rock pools, and possibly anemones too.

Ogmore Down is frequented by the high brown fritillary butterfly, a large distinctively coloured (orange-brown, black and white) butterfly which loves to feed on the flowers of thistles and bramble.

The Ogmore Estuary offers great feeding grounds for wading birds like the sandpiper and greenshank. If you're walking here in winter you'll also see goldeneye ducks.

Greenshank

Heol-y-mynydd

6

2½ miles

Pant Mari Flanders ☆

3 miles

Pant y Cwteri

5 ➽ Take lane signed Heol-y-mynydd to left of farm. This comes to a T-junction by a large green.

6 ➽ Go **straight on**, keeping parallel with boundary on left. Don't stray right on green.
➽ In 100 yards, fork **left**. Path descends into the little valley of Pant Mari Flanders. This opens out into another, Pant y Cwteri, and path veers **right** to B4524.

Top left: dog whelk
and limpets
Top right: sandpiper
Above: goldeneye
Left: high brown fritillary

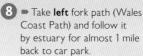

Wales Coast Path

B4524
3½ miles
Portobello
House
4 miles
Ogmore River
4½ miles
Ogmore Beach car park

7 ➡ Pushchairs rejoin
main route.
➡ On reaching the Ogmore
road, **cross** over and take
the waymarked Wales Coast
Path parallel to road (left)
and Ogmore River (right)
past car park to junction by
Portobello House.

8 ➡ Take **left** fork path (Wales
Coast Path) and follow it
by estuary for almost 1 mile
back to car park.

Publishing information

© Crown copyright 2023.
All rights reserved.

Ordnance Survey, OS, and the OS logos are registered trademarks, and OS Short Walks Made Easy is a trademark of Ordnance Survey Ltd.

© Crown copyright and database rights (2023) Ordnance Survey.

ISBN 978 0 319092 63 7
1st edition published by Ordnance Survey 2023.

www.ordnancesurvey.co.uk

While every care has been taken to ensure the accuracy of the route directions, the publishers cannot accept responsibility for errors or omissions, or for changes in details given. The countryside is not static: hedges and fences can be removed, stiles can be replaced by gates, field boundaries can alter, footpaths can be rerouted and changes in ownership can result in the closure or diversion of some concessionary paths. Also, paths that are easy and pleasant for walking in fine conditions may become slippery, muddy and difficult in wet weather.

If you find an inaccuracy in either the text or maps, please contact Ordnance Survey at os.uk/contact.

A catalogue record for this book is available from the British Library.

Milestone Publishing credits

Author: John Gillham

Series editor: Kevin Freeborn

Maps: Cosmographics

Design and Production: Patrick Dawson, Milestone Publishing

Printed in India by Replika Press Pvt. Ltd

MIX
Paper from responsible sources
FSC® C016779
www.fsc.org

Photography credits

Front cover: ©John Gillham. **Back cover** cornfield/Shutterstock.com.

All photographs supplied by the author ©John Gillham except page 6 Chris Knight, Ordnance Survey and pages 1, 33 Kevin Freeborn.

The following images were supplied by Shutterstock.com: pages 5, 17, 23, 33, 62 jax10289; 18, 19 Martin Fowler; 19 Alex Cooper Photography; 19, 38 Sandra Standbridge; 22, 40 Leighton Collins; 24 Gallinago_media; 24 Mateusz Sciborski; 24 TashaBubo; 25 Menno Schaefer; 25 Stephan Morris; 25 thatmacroguy; 32 mariusz.ks; 33 Ms Deborah Waters; 38 COULANGES; 39 Harry Collins Photography; 39 James Hime; 39 Kabar; 40 jennyt; 40 Orlando Tomassini; 40 Richard Bowden; 40 rubacolor; 41 Alexander Piragis; 41 Giedriius; 41 Groomee; 46 Julian Popov; 47 RCB Shooter; 47 Vladimir Wrangel; 52 hecke61; 53 Jerry Gantar; 53 onutancu; 53 Peter Turner Photography; 58 Robert Ruidl; 59 Lois GoBe; 59 Massimiliano Paolino; 59 Risto Puranen; 60 Ian Murdoch; 64 salarko; 66 L-N; 66 marineke thissen; 67 steved_np3; 67 Yuriy Balagula; 73 Andrew Fletcher; 73 Bildagentur Zoonar GmbH; 73 Ger Bosma Photos; 73 rorue; 73 Steven Paul Pepper; 78, 79 Henri_Lehtola; 79 Chris Moody; 79 Edgar Feliz; 79 Paulina Wietrzy-Pelka.

The images on pages 45, 70 are by unknown photographers, Public domain, via Wikimedia Commons.